MARTIN LUTHER KING

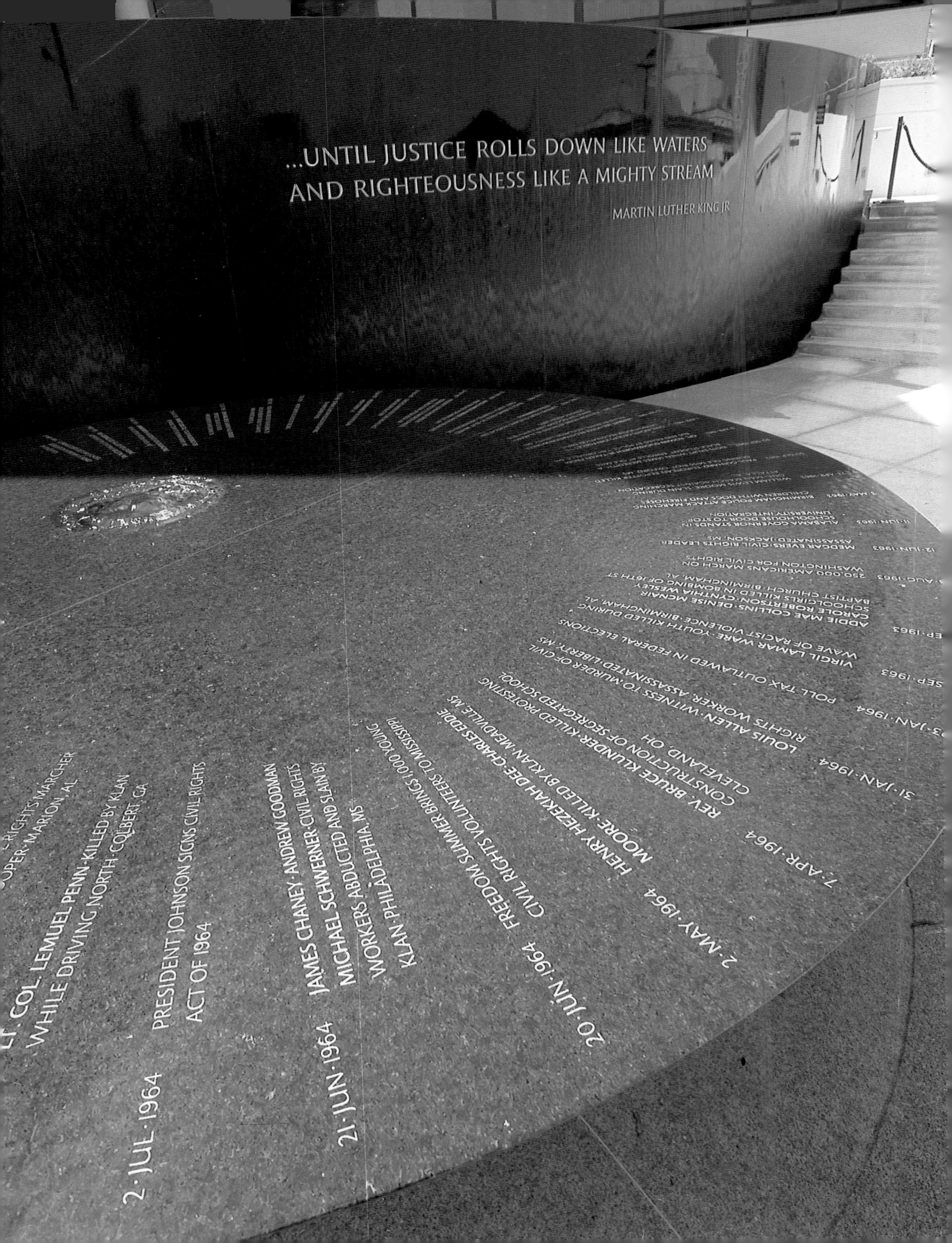

...UNTIL JUSTICE ROLLS DOWN LIKE WATERS
AND RIGHTEOUSNESS LIKE A MIGHTY STREAM

MARTIN LUTHER KING JR

...RIGHTS MARCHER

LT. COL. LEMUEL PENN · KILLED BY KLAN WHILE DRIVING NORTH · COLBERT, GA

2 · JUL · 1964

PRESIDENT JOHNSON SIGNS CIVIL RIGHTS ACT OF 1964

21 · JUN · 1964

JAMES CHANEY · ANDREW GOODMAN · MICHAEL SCHWERNER CIVIL RIGHTS WORKERS ABDUCTED AND SLAIN BY KLAN · PHILADELPHIA, MS

FREEDOM SUMMER BRINGS 1,000 YOUNG CIVIL RIGHTS VOLUNTEERS TO MISSISSIPPI

20 · JUN · 1964

HENRY HEZEKIAH DEE · CHARLES EDDIE MOORE · KILLED BY KLAN · MEADVILLE, MS

2 · MAY · 1964

REV. BRUCE KLUNDER KILLED PROTESTING CONSTRUCTION OF SEGREGATED SCHOOL · CLEVELAND, OH

7 · APR · 1964

LOUIS ALLEN · WITNESS TO MURDER OF CIVIL RIGHTS WORKER · ASSASSINATED · LIBERTY, MS

31 · JAN · 1964

POLL TAX OUTLAWED IN FEDERAL ELECTIONS

23 · JAN · 1964

VIRGIL LAMAR WARE · YOUTH KILLED DURING WAVE OF RACIST VIOLENCE · BIRMINGHAM, AL

SEP · 1963

ADDIE MAE COLLINS · DENISE MCNAIR · CAROLE ROBERTSON · CYNTHIA WESLEY SCHOOLGIRLS KILLED IN BOMBING OF 16TH ST BAPTIST CHURCH · BIRMINGHAM, AL

15 · SEP · 1963

250,000 AMERICANS MARCH ON WASHINGTON FOR CIVIL RIGHTS

28 · AUG · 1963

MEDGAR EVERS · CIVIL RIGHTS LEADER · ASSASSINATED · JACKSON, MS

12 · JUN · 1963

ALABAMA GOVERNOR STANDS IN SCHOOLHOUSE DOOR TO STOP UNIVERSITY INTEGRATION

11 · JUN · 1963

BIRMINGHAM POLICE ATTACK MARCHING CHILDREN WITH DOGS AND FIREHOSES

3 · MAY · 1963

WILLIAM LEWIS MOORE · SLAIN DURING ONE-MAN MARCH AGAINST SEGREGATION

MARTIN LUTHER KING

CHARTWELL
BOOKS, INC.

Published by
CHARTWELL BOOKS
a division of Book Sales, Inc.
Raritan Center
114 Northfield Avenue
Edison, New Jersey 08818

Produced by
Brompton Books Corp.
15 Sherwood Place
Greenwich, Connecticut 06830

ISBN 0-7858-0805-1

Printed in Hong Kong

PAGE 1: Martin Luther King,
Jr. delivers his "I Have a
Dream" speech at the
March on Washington on
August 28, 1963.

PAGE 2: A quote from Martin
Luther King, Jr. graces the
Civil War Memorial in
Montgomery, Alabama.

PAGE 3: King's words and
philosophy fired the Civil
Rights Movement, and his
memory reminds us that,
more than 25 years after
his death, his work is not
yet done.

RIGHT: King leads a civil
rights march through
downtown Detroit,
Michigan, in 1963.

CONTENTS

By the time Alberta and Martin had children, they were doing well financially, and were highly regarded in the community of Atlanta. Christine King was their first child, followed by Martin Luther King, Jr., then Alfred Daniel Williams King III.

In later years, Christine King Farris fondly described the environment that nurtured her and her brothers. Their parents encouraged all of them to strive for excellence and pursuit of knowledge. Like many black people, Martin's family saw education as the key to getting ahead. Money and property could be lost, destroyed or taken away, but not a sound and developed mind.

More than a love and devotion to education was passed on to young Martin. He would become one of a line of ministers who believed that part of the calling of the church was to better black people's lives, not just in the hereafter, but in the here and now.

King's grandfather, Reverend Williams, had been the first president of the National Association for the Advancement of Colored People (NAACP) shortly after its founding in 1910. He worked tirelessly to improve the quality of life for black Atlantans. In an effort to build a black high school, he participated in a drive to defeat local bond

issues until the city agreed to pay for the new high school. When local newspapers mocked African-Americans' striving for equal education, he organized a damaging boycott against them.

Martin King's father, or Daddy King as loved ones called him, continued his father-in-law's agitating as he protested segregation in the South, simultaneously working to improve conditions of black people's lives even as they lived in a segregated system. An influential member of the NAACP and the Atlanta Negro Voters League, he rallied people to desegregate elevators in the Atlanta courthouse. He also organized to equalize salaries of black and white teachers, a fight which he won.

Martin Jr. was an active child who liked playing sports as much as reading. He shared a deep love with his grandmother, Jennie Williams, a religious woman who nurtured his sensitivity and love of spiritual thought and hymns.

Although the love and relative financial ease enjoyed by the King family allowed Martin a certain shelter and comfort, his family could not entirely protect him from the harshness of racism. Martin recalled various incidents that occurred early in his life that forced the ugliness of racism upon him.

FAR LEFT: This man drinks water from a drinking fountain designated for African-Americans. The segregated system of the South, called Jim Crow, included all public facilities. As a result of segregation, blacks created their own schools, churches, businesses and social structure to nurture themselves.

LEFT: Demonstrations such as this anti-lynching march in Washington, D.C., in 1922 gave voice to black people's grievances in Martin Luther King, Jr.'s grandfather's and father's time.

BELOW LEFT: The Reverend Martin Luther King, Sr. was a powerful guiding presence in his son's life.

BELOW: Mrs. Alberta King, Martin's mother, was the official organist at Ebenezer Baptist Church all her life.

LEFT: A 1928 photograph of the members of the National Urban League, formed through a coalition of three organizations in 1910. The NUL set out to help southern blacks who were migrating north to learn to adjust to the urban environment. The organization was interracial from the beginning.

BELOW LEFT: A black proprietor hopes to attract customers with a sign in his window indicating that his store is a "Negro Enterprise."

BELOW: Martin King's alma mater, Morehouse College in Atlanta, Georgia, was founded in 1867.

Until he was 6, Martin played with the white children of a grocer who lived nearby. But at 6, the white children were sent to separate schools, based on color. When Martin went to his friends' house to invite them to play, the parents refused to let them play "because you are colored."

Later, Martin King recalled running home to his mother in tears. She took him into her lap and explained the history of black people in America, telling him that no matter what the white people thought, he was just as good as anybody else.

Years later, King's heart ached as he had to explain to his own weeping daughter Yolanda why the local amusement park Funtown, wasn't open to black families.

Yet another unpleasant childhood incident stuck in Martin's mind. At the age of 14, King won an oratorical contest sponsored by the Negro Elks. The subject was the Negro and the Constitution. Returning from the contest in Dublin, Georgia, Martin and his teacher, Mrs. Bradley, took seats on the bus. A few miles later, some white passengers boarded the bus, and the white driver ordered Martin and his teacher to surrender their seats to the whites. When they didn't jump up immediately, the driver began cursing, calling them "black sons of bitches." Murmuring, "It's the law, Martin," Mrs. Bradley urged Martin to move. They stood in the aisle for the rest of the 90 miles to Atlanta. King later remembered that night as the angriest he had ever been in his life. Thirteen years later, that anger fed one of the most powerful shows of solidarity ever seen in the United States.

Upon finishing eleventh grade, Martin gained admission to Morehouse College in Atlanta. Morehouse was an exciting place to be because debate on racial issues of the day were openly encouraged. Dr. Benjamin E. Mays, the president of Morehouse and a passionate crusader against segregation, saw the role of the black universities as places to foster debate, thought, and action on black-white equality. At prestigious, all-male Morehouse, nicknamed the "Negro Harvard," students sat up late discussing the pressing issues of the day such as segregation, and the role of leadership for the young men that were graduated from Morehouse.

Dr. Benjamin Mays played a mentoring role in King's life, the intensity of which King revealed when he wrote

LEFT: The Reverend Dr. Benjamin E. Mays, scholar, civic leader, and president of Morehouse College, was one of young Martin King's mentors.

Stride Toward Freedom (1958), his account of the Montgomery Bus Boycott. Mays visited the King household often, held informal chats with Martin on campus, and remained willing to discuss questions and challenges posed by Martin after Mays's Tuesday morning lecture on faith and spirituality.

Although an avid student, Martin was not always serious. His younger brother A.D. remembered that Martin especially loved to dance and socialize with the ladies. In fact, he was one of the best jitterbuggers around when he was a teenager. A fastidious dresser, he wore tweed suits so often that he earned the nickname "Tweed."

At first, Martin King had no desire to follow in the footsteps of his grandfather and father by joining the ministry. Instead, he wanted to be a lawyer or a doctor, believing these to be better professions to enter in order to serve his people. He loved the intellectual nature of the law, and did not know if he could find rigorous scholarship and intellectual stimulation in the ministry. Yet the influence of Benjamin Mays and Dr. George D. Kelsey, both seminary-trained ministers whose sermons were socially relevant and intellectually stimulating, helped Martin to see how

he could combine the emotional depth of the ministry with intellect.

So he decided to join the ministry.

He entered Crozer Theological Seminary, in Chester, Pennsylvania, and earned a Bachelors Degree in Divinity. Despite his father's comments that this was all he needed to come back to Atlanta to preach, he went on to Boston University School of Theology to earn his Ph.D.

While King was in Boston, Mary Powell, a friend from the South, introduced him to Coretta Scott. Coretta, who was born on a farm a few miles outside of Marion, Alabama, had also journeyed far from home. After earning a teaching degree in elementary-level music education, she decided to deepen her study of music, and go to the New England Conservatory of Music. Marriage was far from Coretta's mind, for her desire to pursue her art was great. Young Martin called her. In her book, *My Life with Martin Luther King, Jr.*, Coretta recalled the baritone's silken words: "You know every Napoleon has his Waterloo. I'm like Napoleon. I'm at my Waterloo, and I'm on my knees."

She agreed to a date, and the two of them found much that they enjoyed and respected in one another. After the

ABOVE: Coretta Scott with classmates at Antioch College, Yellow Springs, Ohio. Elementary school education majors were required to do a year of practice teaching in the Yellow Springs, Ohio, public school system. Yet, public school officials would not allow her to teach because she was black. Antioch refused to press the issue. While a bitter experience, it fired her determination to clear the path for others, and she became active in the NACCP, a race relations committee and a civil liberties committee while in college.

RIGHT: In June 1955, Martin was awarded his Ph.D. from Boston University School of Theology. He was 26 years old.

first date, moved by Coretta's loving and intelligent nature, Martin looked deep into her eyes, and told her that she was the kind of woman he wanted to marry. They courted for a year, during which time Coretta searched deep within her heart to decide if Martin was the man for her. They were married on June 18, 1953, with Daddy King presiding.

When Martin King finished school at the Boston University School of Theology, he started looking for a church to minister. Both Coretta and Martin wanted to return to the South, for despite the reality of Jim Crow there, the caring and nurturing among the people of the southern black community created a world they dearly loved and missed. Martin's father invited him to return to Atlanta and preach at Ebenezer Baptist Church. However, wanting to strike out on his own, Martin accepted an offer to preach at Dexter Avenue Baptist Church in Montgomery, Alabama. Dexter was a small, well-to-do church, full of many professional, highly educated black people. The former pastor, Vernon Johns, had been a firebrand, who spoke so savagely and plainly against segregation and lynchings that white people threatened his safety. As a result of the controversy, and the possibility that he might bring trouble down on his congregation, the congregation sometimes questioned the wisdom of his deeds. Johns finally resigned.

Upon taking the reins at Dexter Avenue, King set about asserting his authority as the new pastor. He had barely been pastor one year when Rosa Parks refused to leave her seat on a bus.

LEFT: Dexter Avenue Baptist Church, in Montgomery, Alabama, offered the young Martin King a pastorship. This plaque celebrates the church's distinguished past.

RIGHT: The elite Dexter Avenue Baptist Church had a reputation for being hard on its ministers. Martin made clear from the start that he planned to be an authoritative pastor.

CHAPTER 2

BOYCOTTING THE BUSES

The Montgomery Bus Boycott of 1955-56 had been a long time coming. Long before Martin Luther King, Jr. arrived, the women of Montgomery had already had enough. Most of the riders of Montgomery's segregated buses were black women on their way to work in rich white women's homes.

Day after day they suffered the indignity of white bus drivers who cursed them, demanding that they surrender their seats to white people or face arrest. Even when they obeyed the bus drivers, sometimes they still suffered. In order to sit in the back of the bus, the black rider stepped off the bus after paying in front, and reboarded in back. Mean-spirited drivers sometimes just drove off, leaving the rider standing outside after having paid.

One of the groups that organized to address the injustices toward black people in Montgomery was the Women's Political Council, started by Mary Fair Burks in 1946. By 1955, Jo Ann Robinson was spearheading the Council's activities. The WPC had discussed a boycott of the buses for a while, coming up with a proposal for how to make the bus system more fair. They proposed a first-come, first-served seating policy, with black people filling in the seats from back to front, and whites filling in the seats from front to back. They also wanted to be treated courteously by the bus drivers. Now the women awaited the perfect person to challenge the existing system.

Today, Rosa Parks is well known as the one who refused to give up her seat, but the fact is that Rosa Parks was just one in a long line of black women who refused to give up their seats. Years before the ground-breaking Brown vs. Board of Education court decision that stated that segregated school systems were unequal, Viola White nearly beat a driver to death who tried to force her to move. And just a few weeks before Rosa Parks refused to give up her seat, another woman refused. At first glance, it looked as if this woman might be the test case. But on further investigation, the WPC found that the young woman was pregnant and unmarried. Fearing that she'd be torn apart by public scrutiny, the WPC let it go.

Not only was Rosa Parks a hard-working seamstress, she was also a former secretary of the NAACP. And just two weeks earlier, she had attended a workshop at Highlander Center on school desegregation.

Years later, Rosa recalled the bus driver standing over her, telling her to get up and make room for a white man to sit down. Rosa was in the section of the bus that was reserved for black people, unless a white person demanded that seat. And since black and white could not sit side by side, if a white person sat in one seat on a row, that whole row must be emptied of black people. When she asked the bus driver, "Why do you treat us so bad?" he replied, "I do not know, but it's the law." The police took her away.

As news of Rosa Parks's arrest spread, the women of

RIGHT: Blacks in the back, whites in the front: the Montgomery Bus Boycott was organized to put an end to segregation.

the WPC sprang into action. Edward Daniel (E.D.) Nixon, an influential activist in the radical black union the Brotherhood of Sleeping Car Porters and Maids, rushed to the police station to sign bail for Rosa Parks. Once Nixon and the WPC decided that Rosa Parks would be the test case, he called around to the ministers in town to inform them to decide on a meeting place. Since Nixon had to do a run on the railroad, he wasn't able to hold a meeting at his church. He called the Reverend Martin Luther King, Jr., to ask him to hold it at Dexter Avenue Baptist Church. At first Martin said no, but then on second thought, he agreed.

During the Friday meeting, it was decided that a boycott should begin on Monday morning, December 5th, and that a mass meeting must be held on the evening of the 5th so that people could speak their minds, and decide together how long a boycott should continue. The women of the WPC mimeographed and distributed 50,000 flyers throughout the black community of Montgomery. Even

the newspaper helped to spread the word, after Nixon's call to a sympathetic journalist who published word of the boycott in the *Montgomery Advertiser*.

Coretta King recalled proudly standing together with Martin in front of their window on that first morning of the boycott, waiting anxiously for the first bus to roll around the corner. At four o'clock a.m., the first bus came ambling down the street – empty! This bus was usually jammed with black women going to their jobs across town. Martin jumped in his car, and started driving around town to see if that sight was being repeated across town. It was.

That night, the mass meeting was held at the Holt Street Baptist Church. The steering committee for the boycott had elected Martin Luther King to be the president of the new group, which they named, at activist Ralph Abernathy's suggestion, the Montgomery Improvement Association. At first reluctant, King refused the position. He and Coretta had just given birth to their first child,

LEFT: Rosa Parks and E. D. Nixon (left) speak to reporters about the Montgomery Bus Boycott in March 1956.

ABOVE: (Left to right) Reverend Ralph Abernathy, Reverend Garner, Rufus Lewis, Reverend L. R. Bennett, Reverend W. F. Alford, Reverend J. H. Cherry, Reverend H. H.

Herbert and Eli Judkins were jailed for organizing the boycott on February 22, 1956.

RIGHT: Martin Luther King, Jr. and Coretta Scott King leave the Montgomery County Courthouse on March 19, 1956 after facing charges of illegally inciting a boycott.

Yolanda. In addition, new duties at his church made him feel pressured to put all his efforts into doing his best there. But he realized that he had a responsibility to help the Montgomery citizens make a change, so he was persuaded. The call had been issued. King answered with full heart.

To prepare for that night's meeting, Martin had 20 minutes to write a speech that would inspire people to continue the boycott until they obtained results. In *Stride Toward Freedom*, he describes his fear and sense of inadequacy. He searched for words that would fire people up to stand firm, yet not so incense them that they would become combative.

Hundreds packed the church, with thousands lining the streets. The service started with the soul-stirring hymn, "Onward Christian Soldiers," followed by scripture reading and prayer. When introduced, the 26-year-old King stood up. Thin, barely looking his age, he began to speak, his words flowing in that melodic fashion that would

become world-famous. He described the incident that had happened to Rosa, affirming the indignities that the black people had suffered for so long. He explained the boycott in both a moral and legal framework, stressing that as citizens of the United States they were in line with the profound truism of democracy which is "the right to protest for right." He called on the people to take a stand, to boycott the buses, in the spirit of upholding justice and the moral right. He pleaded with them not to shun those that disobeyed the boycott in good conscience. He ended with a call that the people take this step in the spirit of Christian love, and promised that when the history books were written, they would praise the contribution of the black people who reminded white America of the true meaning of democracy.

The audience voted to boycott the buses until the bus company agreed to treat blacks courteously, hire black bus drivers on routes used mostly by black people, and uphold a first-come, first-served seating policy with blacks in the back, and whites in the front.

At first people travelled to work in carpools and taxis. The boycott organizers arranged for black taxi companies to transport people for the cost of the bus ride, 10 cents. When the city officials issued an order that forbade taxi companies to charge less than 45 cents, the MIA came up with another solution. They organized a fleet of cars, set up dispatch stations, and raised the funds to buy station wagons to transport the people. Members of the community – ministers, teachers, housewives – volunteered to take turns driving. And many people simply walked – four or five miles to work, and back again.

Even the white women who employed many of the black women as maids helped. Because they weren't about to be without their servants, they drove them to and from work.

Weekly meetings at the churches helped fortify people's spirits and spread information about new developments during the boycott.

King and the MIA did not think that the boycott would last as long as it did. The requests that they were making were not unprecedented in the South. Other communities had agreed to these demands on their buses, for they were not asking for integration. However, the Montgomery officials and bus company were adamant that they would make no concessions. So the MIA decided to demand full integration. They filed a suit with the United States Federal District Court asking for an end to bus segregation on the basis that it contradicted the Fourteenth Amendment.

As biographer David Garrow points out, part of what made King so able to answer the call to lead was a spiritual

LEFT: Like the buses, waiting areas in Montgomery were also segregated.

RIGHT: The year-long Montgomery Bus Boycott is over. These two men choose seats in whatever part of the bus they want after the November 1956 Supreme Court ruling banning segregation on the buses takes effect.

NOTICE

IT IS REQUIRED BY LAW UNDER
PENALTY OF FINE OF $5⁰⁰ TO $25⁰⁰
THAT WHITE AND NEGRO PASSENGERS MUST
OCCUPY THE RESPECTIVE SPACE OR SEATS
INDICATED BY SIGNS IN THIS VEHICLE

TEXAS PENAL CODE. ARTICLE 1659 SEC 4
DALLAS CITY ORDINANCE NO 2904

COLORED →

awakening that occurred during the seventh week of the Montgomery Bus Boycott. King described that night in his account, *Stride Toward Freedom.* Martin was weary. He had been arrested for the first time, and his phone rang constantly with ugly messages and death threats. Reflecting on the first 25 years of his life, he mulled over the happiness and security that he had always known. Whenever he had a problem, he could call on his father, and he hadn't needed to work to survive. Even his religion had been handed to him. But that night, around midnight, weary and feeling that he could go on no longer, knowing that not even his mother and father could rescue him from this frightening situation, he realized that his religion must become truly his. And in that abyss of despair, he prayed. He prayed for understanding, and for guidance, and for strength. And Martin King felt his prayer answered. He felt the Lord say to him, "Martin Luther, stand up for righteousness, stand up for justice, stand up for truth." And in that instant, he felt the Lord promise to stay with him always. This awakening was to be reinforced in the years to come, as King called on the Lord in prayer and meditation, profoundly believing that the Lord would never leave him.

Just one week later, King's house was bombed while he was at a weekly rally in the church. Coretta, a friend, and little Yolanda were in the house. Fortunately, they were unharmed. When Martin learned what happened, he rushed home, accompanied by many of the people who had been at the service. People broiled with anger. Martin stood before them on his porch, hand outstretched. He begged them to fight with love, channelling this anger into the boycott. The people dispersed.

As news of the boycott spread around the country, support poured in. Contributions came from NAACP chapters around the country, from the United Automobile Workers, and from thousands of individuals. In 1955, a group called In Friendship was formed by Bayard Rustin, Stanley Levison and Ella Baker to raise money for people suffering reprisals for taking a stand politically. One of the ways they raised money for the MIA was a 1956 rally in Madison Square Garden.

On November 13, 1956, the federal Supreme Court upheld a ruling banning segregation on the buses, on the grounds that it was unconstitutional. Black citizens of Montgomery voted to end the boycott in December 1956.

As black people boarded the buses to ride in the front, a festive spirit of victory and triumph took them over. Jo

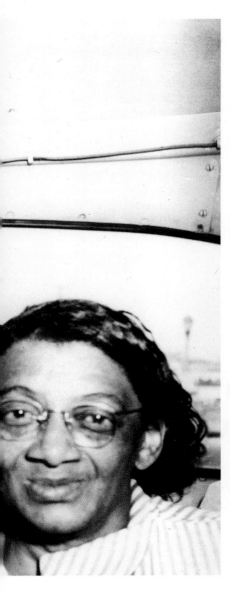

ABOVE: These women in Dallas, Texas, celebrate the pending removal of the segregation signs in the buses after the Supreme Court ruling that banned segregation.

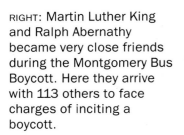

RIGHT: Martin Luther King and Ralph Abernathy became very close friends during the Montgomery Bus Boycott. Here they arrive with 113 others to face charges of inciting a boycott.

LEFT: Rosa Parks, whose arrest on December 1, 1955 triggered the Montgomery Bus Boycott, rides in the front of the bus to celebrate the boycott's success.

RIGHT: King with his mother, Alberta King, and Coretta Scott King as he recovers from a stabbing by Izola Curry. Curry was later found to be deranged.

BELOW RIGHT: Mahatma Mohandas Gandhi leads thousands in a 200-mile march in protest of a statute establishing a government salt monopoly in 1930. Deeply moved by Gandhi's tenets of non-violence, King travelled to India in 1959 to learn more about his philosophy and work.

Ann Robinson of the WPC called it a "hilarious feeling." "It makes you feel that America is a great place and we're going to do more to make it greater."

The Montgomery Bus Boycott victory thrust Martin Luther King, Jr. and the example of black people organizing non-violently on a massive scale into the national spotlight. King's book *Stride Toward Freedom* documented many of the steps taken to reach that victory. While King was signing books on a national tour, Ms. Izola Curry plunged a steel letter opener into his heart. By sitting perfectly still, barely breathing, King had prevented the sharp weapon from cutting through the aorta and ending his life.

During this time, King wrote a monthly column for *Ebony* magazine. Soon after the stabbing incident, a reader wrote to ask Martin how he maintained such grace and belief in non-violence after being stabbed. He replied that he constantly prayed to God to remove all bitterness from his heart, and to provide him with the strength to face any troubles that confronted him. King believed deeply in the creative power of love and constructive non-violence to transform society. He believed that the very act of engaging in non-violence and suffering the attacks that followed changed the heart of the oppressed, by causing that person to draw on reserves of strength and courage that he or she never knew existed. Finally the opponent's heart was touched, and in being so touched, the space for reconciliation opened.

The success in Montgomery showed King that the philosophy of constructive non-violence and the power of

ABOVE LEFT: Coretta speaks with students from around the world who are attending India's Delhi College.

LEFT: King speaks with Sucheta Kripalani and Acharya Kripalani, activists in the India independence movement.

ABOVE: King pauses for a photograph after a meeting with Indian president Jawaharlal Nehru (second from right). Also shown are King's biographer Lawrence Reddick (left), and Coretta.

Mahatma Mohandas Gandhi's massive show of non-violent organizing as a way to gain Indian independence. When the Gandhi Memorial Trust Fund and the American Friends Service Committee (AFSC) agreed to co-sponsor a trip to India, King leapt at the chance. On March 1959, Martin, Coretta, and Lawrence Reddick, King's biographer, enplaned for India.

Escorted by James Bristol, the AFSC Quaker Service representative in India, the Kings and Reddick met with some of the most prestigious and influential Indians of the day.

They met Minister Jawaharlal Nehru, the political leader of the Independence movement. Nehru impressed Martin with the depth of his social conscience. They also met Indira Gandhi, who became the prime minister in 1966, and again in 1980.

They met with Vinoba Bhave, a meeting that especially excited Dr. King because Vinoba was working to get landowners to give up their land voluntarily, so that those without land would have a place to live and farm. Bhave saw government as corrupt, and envisioned a system of *sarvodaya* – a spiritual, decentralized socialism.

They travelled to Gandhigram (Gandhi Village), a non-violence training center in southern India. During prayer

truth developed and made famous by the great Indian nationalist, Mahatma Gandhi, could work in the United States. During the boycott, Fellowship of Reconciliation workers Bayard Rustin and Glen Smiley contributed to Martin's understanding of non-violence. His hunger to understand the workings of Gandhi had been growing since his college days, when he heard Mordecai Johnson's description of Gandhi's non-violent struggle to free India from colonial rule.

For years King had wanted to travel to India, the site of

meetings, scriptures were read from Hindu, Muslim, Christian and Buddhist sources. At all the ashrams, King's love of children shone. The children loved hanging onto Martin's arms and hands, following him everywhere.

Tina Bristol, James Bristol's daughter, recalls Martin and Coretta King as ordinary people, made extraordinary by their passionate commitment to justice. She remembers that every word that Martin uttered was either profoundly weighty, or hilariously funny. He'd make jokes about going to jail, and turn the sad intransigence of the white racists that they faced on their marches into funny stories, pointing out the foolishness and foibles of their way of seeing the world. Tina is one of many who remembers King's sense of humor, and ability to make light in rough moments.

She remembers the radiant beauty of Coretta, a beauty

LEFT: While in India, King addressed numerous groups. Just as he was hungry to learn about non-violence in the India independence movement, Indians wanted to learn more about non-violence in the struggle for equality for African-Americans.

BELOW: AFSC workers and hosts for the Kings, Jim Bristol and daughter Tina (far left) watch Lawrence Reddick and the Kings honor Gandhi by placing a wreath on Gandhi's shrine.

that transcended the external, emanating from within. Everywhere they went, Coretta sang African-American spirituals, her lovely voice and the message of the songs drawing the Indian people closer to the lives of the black people in the United States. Coretta was taken to the All-India Radio studios to hear Indian music and see a display of Indian musical instruments. She was inspired by the role women played in achieving Indian independence, for many of the women had sacrificed and gone to prison just as the men did. In fact, Mahatma Gandhi had appreciated and encouraged their participation.

While inspired by the progress that independent India had made in addressing issues such as that of the "untouchables" (the caste system there had been banned), the Kings were heartbroken and shocked at the extent of poverty in India. Upon their return to the United States, both Martin and Coretta described the appalling poverty of thousands of homeless, emaciated people lugging the bundles that contained all their belongings.

In addition to listening and learning while in India, Martin shared his understanding of non-violence and what it meant for African-Americans. He described the suffering and victories of African-Americans, and praised the Indian people for embracing non-violence. He asked that Indian people continue to lead the world with their example of non-violence, and unilaterally disarm. As early as 1959, Martin was talking about the importance of nuclear disarmament as an important aspect of maintaining peace.

CHAPTER 3

CONFRONTATION IN BIRMINGHAM

After the Montgomery campaign, King pondered how to continue the struggle that had been so widely publicized and had resulted in the desegregation of the buses. Black people in Montgomery, Alabama, as well as in other states throughout the country, still faced tremendous violence through police brutality, anonymous bombings and lynchings, and the steady degradation of spirit. In order to address these national problems, King and his dear friend and associate, the Reverend Ralph Abernathy, combined forces with a group of ministers to create the Southern Christian Leadership Conference (SCLC) in 1957.

The SCLC's goal was to integrate black people into all areas of American life. They set up plans to stimulate non-violent, direct mass action in order to expose and eliminate segregation and discrimination, lead workshops on the how and why of non-violence, and make sure that every citizen had the opportunity to vote. In order to help blacks fully participate in society as voting, critical thinkers, they adopted the powerful model of citizenship schools made successful by Septima Clark and the Highlander Center in Tennessee.

Drawing on past experiences, King and the SCLC developed a series of strategies that they used in their campaigns. One of these strategies was to wait until asked before entering a community. Martin explained that that way they knew that a community was already organized and would benefit from the national attention and assistance that came from the SCLC's involvement. The SCLC also wanted to make sure that the condition was so critical that national attention would expose the intolerable conditions that blacks were enduring, leading to change.

Birmingham, Alabama, was ripe for the involvement of the SCLC in 1963. With everything from public facilities to city parks segregated, Birmingham was also a very violent city for black people to live in. Between 1957 and 1963, there were 50 cross burnings, and 18 racially motivated bombings. Only one-eighth of those on the voting rolls were black people, even though black people comprised two-thirds of the population. The NAACP was illegal, having been declared a foreign corporation by state officials.

The Reverend Fred Shuttlesworth, an energetic and forceful man, organized the Alabama Christian Movement for Human Rights (ACMHR) in Birmingham in 1956. Weekly mass meetings drew a consistent body of people willing to take a stand to change the city's segregationist policies. Collections gathered at these meetings funded the actions taken by the ACMHR. People trusted the Reverend Shuttlesworth because he and his wife had demonstrated their commitment to making change in Birmingham, no matter what the personal cost. In an effort to desegregate schools, Shuttlesworth and his wife escorted their children to the Birmingham high school. Angered whites and members of the Ku Klux Klan attacked and beat them with chains, stabbing Mrs. Shuttlesworth in the hip. This didn't stop them.

Shuttlesworth and the ACMHR had led battles in the courts and led boycotts on the streets. When the ACMHR won one battle against the city over the segregation of public recreation facilities, the city closed the city parks rather than have black and white children playing together. Shuttlesworth and the ACMHR also launched boy-

LEFT: The Civil Rights Movement exposed the nation to the violence that black people lived with daily. Here King holds his son Martin III and looks at a cross burned by the Ku Klux Klan in the front yard of his Atlanta, Georgia, home in 1960.

BELOW: Septima Clark and Rosa Parks at Highlander Center in Tennessee. A radical, interracial training center for social change activists, Highlander taught people how to become responsible movers in their communities. Septima Clark headed Highlander's education program in the 1950s, and designed the Citizenship Schools that the SCLC used as a model for democratic movement building.

cotts of certain local businesses which refused to serve black customers, or which only hired black people for the most menial work. Shuttlesworth was jailed several times, and his home and church were bombed. The actions of the ACMHR and Shuttlesworth paved the way for the SCLC to come into Birmingham.

After careful consideration, the SCLC decided to go into Birmingham. As King says in his book *Why We Can't Wait* (1963), he hoped forcing a confrontation in Birmingham over segregation could provide the impetus to break the back of segregation throughout the South.

Drawing on lessons learned from a disillusioning campaign in Albany, Georgia, King and the SCLC decided to be very specific in their approach in Birmingham. The SCLC had entered Albany, Georgia, at the invitation of Dr.

William G. Anderson, one of the organizers of that effort to desegregate the city. However, even after a long struggle, they did not achieve their goals. From that bitter disappointment, King learned that targeting business is more effective than targeting City Hall. He believed that once merchants were hurt financially, they would put pressure on city officials to change laws.

With this in mind, the SCLC targeted Birmingham's business community, building on the ACMHR's boycotts of companies that discriminated against and mistreated black people. Striving to maintain a unified front, they persuaded much of the black leadership to join with them.

The Birmingham campaign, called Project Confrontation, began on April 3, 1963. It started with sit-ins at lunch counters where store owners refused to allow black

LEFT: The Reverend Fred Shuttlesworth (right) leads demonstrators in prayer before setting out to protest segregation in Birmingham.

RIGHT: Surrounded by police are (left to right) Martin King, Ralph Abernathy, and Dr. William Anderson, president of the Albany movement. In Albany, Georgia, lack of coordinated efforts between local people and the SCLC resulted in defeat.

LEFT: Abernathy and King march in Birmingham in defiance of a court order forbidding demonstrations. They and 51 others were arrested on Good Friday, April 12, 1963.

RIGHT: King ponders next steps while waiting in his jail cell in Jefferson County Courthouse, Birmingham, Alabama.

people to eat. Although black people were permitted to shop at these stores, they could not rest over lunch after shopping. After the protesters sat for a while, the police would come and arrest them.

The next part of the plan was to continue the mass rallies. The meetings started with freedom songs, then went on to a program of prayer and inspirational pep talks. At the end of the meeting, arms outstretched, King invited people to join the non-violent army. Volunteers underwent intensive non-violent training programs that prepared them through dramatizations and enactments to deal with attacks on their person.

On April 10, 1963, the city obtained a state injunction ordering that all boycotts and demonstrations cease. In addition, the SCLC was almost out of money for posting bail. Hundreds of people were in jail, and without money SCLC couldn't get them released. Many of the people couldn't afford to be away from work, and not having money meant that many of the adults wouldn't be willing to get arrested because they had too many financial and domestic responsibilities.

King did not know what to do. Andrew Young, one of King's aides, recalled the tension of that moment, and the sense of doom that fell over the Gaston Motel room as King and his companions puzzled over their next moves. King went off to pray alone. He emerged in about a half-hour, dressed in jeans. He said, "We're going to jail." He

added that he didn't know what would happen next, but that maybe if he joined the people in jail, something would come to him.

On Good Friday, a symbolic day because of Jesus Christ's arrest, King led a march to City Hall, purposely violating the state injunction. He was arrested, together with Ralph Abernathy and 49 others. Placed in solitary confinement, he was not allowed to have a private meeting with his lawyer, or to make phone calls

On Easter Sunday, April 14, Coretta had reached the end of her rope. Unable to reach her husband, she called the singer Harry Belafonte, who offered to pay for a secretary and nurse for the children so that Coretta could go to Birmingham. Belafonte, a staunch supporter of King and the SCLC, was busy raising money for the SCLC to cover bail costs. He successfully raised $50,000 that weekend.

Coretta began her efforts to track down her husband by calling the White House. Having no success, she followed that call with a call to press secretary Pierre Salinger, who promised to pass her message to the president. Not an hour later, Attorney General Robert Kennedy responded to her call, and said that he would see to it that King was all right. The next afternoon, President Kennedy called Coretta to say that he was concerned about the situation, and had been able to find out that King was indeed safe.

While in jail, King decided to respond to eight clergy-

men who were angrily criticizing him for his actions. Reflecting the thoughts of other moderate whites in Birmingham, they deplored the fact that King had not waited to see if the new government that had been sworn in on April 2, 1963, might not do something different from the preceding government.

Angered and distressed, King responded by writing in the margins of newspapers and on toilet paper. Smuggled out of jail, the letter came to be know as the "Letter from Birmingham Jail." In the letter, King explained why the black community could afford to wait no longer. He reminded these clergymen that attempts to negotiate with business leaders had been made in the prior year, resulting in promises the business leaders carelessly broke. To answer accusations that he was creating a crisis, he replied that non-violent direct action works by revealing that which is already there. This crisis now forced those in power to confront the situation head on and to resolve it, instead of making empty promises. Eloquently naming the particulars of injustice, from being called "boy" and "nigger" to having to explain to your little girl why she cannot go to a whites-only amusement park, to seeing your loved ones twisted and warped by poverty in the belly of an affluent society, King made clear why 340 years of injustice was waiting long enough. He ended his letter with a challenge to these ministers, and by default to ministers

TOP LEFT: On May 6, 1963, children stayed home from school to protest segregated facilities throughout Birmingham. Here they begin the march from the Sixteenth Street Baptist Church.

LEFT: The children did not get far. They walked only one block before police herded them into police vans and took them to jail. Hundreds were arrested that day in the biggest civil rights demonstration the South had ever seen.

ABOVE: Police Commissioner Eugene "Bull" Connor leads police officers in arresting demonstrators.

around the country, to live up to the radical beginnings of Christianity, a religion founded with the energy of transformation.

Seven days later, King got out of jail. While waiting for the ruling on his disobeying the state injunction, he and the SCLC planned their next action.

On May 2nd, the event that shook the nation began. Young people began to march to City Hall. Hundreds of children stayed out of school so that they could march. They started at Sixteenth Street Baptist Church, and the first column was arrested by Commissioner of Police Eugene "Bull" Connor and his troops before reaching City Hall. Then a second column started out, and a third, all of them arrested. By evening Birmingham police had arrested more than 700 children.

The next day, children began gathering at the church again to resume marching. Bull Connor authorized police to blockade church exits so that the young people couldn't reach City Hall. The 500 or so that got out were assaulted by dogs, nightsticks and powerful streams of water from firehoses. The streams of water, 100 pounds of pressure per square inch, were so powerful that they caved in people's rib cages and tore off their clothes.

Coverage of the assault on the children shocked the nation. Coverage even extended around the globe. Telegrams assailed the White House. Until the Children's Crusade, President Kennedy had tried to intervene as little as possible in Birmingham and had sent Assistant Attorney General Burke Marshall there to hammer out an accord, to no avail. Now Kennedy realized that he must take stronger action and order federal intervention.

LEFT: In order to break up the demonstrators, police bring out the dogs.

RIGHT: A young man is swept along the street by a stream of water from fire hoses manned by firemen fighting the demonstrators.

BELOW RIGHT: During the 3000-strong rally, these three hold hands for strength against the battering torrents of water.

BELOW: Firemen unleash streams of water under high pressure to turn back the columns of demonstrators.

Business leaders in Birmingham also wanted an agreement. They had lost a lot of money because of the boycotts and unrest, and realized that they must make concessions. On May 10, 1963, an accord was reached between business leaders, civic officials and the black community which answered the demands of the black community.

The result, however, was not instant peace. That night, bombs were thrown into the Gaston Motel, where the SCLC organized; into A.D. King's house; and into other leaders' homes. Angry black people responded with fighting in the streets that lasted for hours.

King didn't want to let up on President Kennedy or Congress. Believing deeply that there was a national mandate for civil rights legislation, he wracked his brain for a way to show it. He and the heads of other organizations, including A. Philip Randolph of the Negro American Labor Council, Roy Wilkens of the NAACP, John Lewis of the Student Non-violent Coordinating Committee (SNCC), Dorothy Height of the National Council of Negro Women, James Farmer of the Congress of Racial Equality (CORE), and Whitney Young of the Urban League, came up with the idea of a march on Washington. A. Philip Randolph had been dreaming about a march on Washington for years. In 1941, he used the threat of a national march on Washington to pressure President Franklin D. Roosevelt to establish the Fair Employment Practices Committee to address the exclusion of blacks from jobs in the defense industries.

Now, the time had come. With Bayard Rustin as

ABOVE: More than 200,000 people participated in the March on Washington for Jobs and Freedom held on August 28, 1963. People marched from the Washington Monument to the Lincoln Memorial, shown here.

RIGHT: Participants included civil right organizations, community groups, unions and individuals.

ABOVE LEFT: This effigy of King hangs from a tree at the National Headquarters of the National States Rights Party in Birmingham.

LEFT: (Left to right) Shuttlesworth, Abernathy and King announce the success of demonstrations and boycotts to abolish segregation and increase employment of black people in Birmingham businesses.

Deputy Director of the march, Randolph set about organizing it. People were mobilized throughout the nation to participate in a non-violent demonstration in Washington, D.C., demanding jobs, freedom, and sweeping civil rights legislation.

King and the organizers hoped for 100,000 people. Their joy was boundless as over 250,000 people, white and black, made the symbolic walk from the Washington Monument to Lincoln Memorial on August 28, 1963. Speakers included the Reverend Fred Shuttlesworth, A. Philip Randolph, and John Lewis, and between speeches, well-known artists sang freedom songs. Martin Luther King spoke last.

Taking in the throng before him, King celebrated that the march showed that whites were awakening to the fact that their destiny was inextricably linked to the freedom of black people.

Calling on blacks to continue to reach for the finest in themselves, he beseeched them to turn away from the cup of bitterness and hatred, and rise to meet physical force with soul force.

In his speech, which has come to be known as the "I Have a Dream" speech, he challenged America to live up to the promises made in the Declaration of Independence and the Constitution that all men had the right to life,

ABOVE LEFT: King gave his famous "I have a Dream" speech at the March on Washington. Although he prepared beforehand, the excitement of the moment led him to improvise a great deal of the speech.

ABOVE: The power of King's charisma and caring energy was so strong that people always longed to touch him.

LEFT: People listen to speakers at the Lincoln Memorial.

liberty and the pursuit of happiness. He warned America that black people would not settle for less than full justice. America had presented black people with a "bad check," and they refused to accept that the "Bank of Justice" was empty.

Citing the injustices that black people faced in various states of the Union, he warned that there would be no peace until police brutality ended; until mobility did not mean moving from a smaller ghetto to a larger one; until all blacks had access to the vote; and until segregation no longer stripped black children of their dignity.

"No," he thundered, "No, we are not satisfied, and we will not be satisfied until justice rolls down like waters and righteousness like a mighty stream."

The March on Washington proved to be a mixed blessing. For many civil rights leaders, it was one of the high points of their lives. Yet other organizers viewed it as a show to make Kennedy look good before the international community, as speakers praised him for proposing the Civil Rights Bill. To that end, speaker John Lewis of the SNCC was pressured to eliminate any criticisms of Kennedy from his speech.

Despite its shortcomings, the March on Washington, the largest demonstration ever in the nation's capital, stunned the nation as an unprecedented show of black and white unity within the United States.

CHAPTER 4

SELMA AND THE BALLOT

After the Birmingham campaign, mass sit-ins and demonstrations erupted in 800 southern cities. Pressure was so great on President Kennedy that he proposed sweeping civil rights legislation to Congress. The Civil Rights Act of 1964 did not pass until after Kennedy's death. A potent bill, it banned discrimination in employment, secured equal access to public accommodations, and provided the federal government with the authority to enforce these laws.

Tragedy followed the Birmingham campaign as well. In September, Birmingham once again showed why black people nicknamed it "Bombingham." Sixteenth Street Church was bombed while people prepared for worship. The bomb ripped a hole through the wall of the church, and four young girls were killed. The church had been a center for rallies and marching during the campaign. White extremists were determined to make clear that the cost of rebellion was high.

The bombing fed a continual question that King had to deal with from critics – whether black people were bringing the violence onto themselves. In reply to such criticisms, King simply pointed out that whenever oppressed people stand up for themselves, there is a re-action which often takes the form of violence. Yet the oppressed are inevitably blamed for the violence done against them.

King's commitment to his work was all-consuming, and he spent long times away from home. Introducing a 1965 interview with King, *Playboy* magazine reported that he worked at least 20 hours a day and travelled 325,000 miles and made 450 speeches per year speaking out for justice for African-Americans. He had been jailed fourteen times, had his home bombed three times, and received at least one death threat per day.

He received numerous praises and awards for his dedication, ranging from honorary degrees to being named Man of the Year by *Time* magazine. On December 10, 1964, he received the Nobel Peace Prize. The youngest recipient ever, and only the second African-American, King accepted the prize as a representative of the Civil Rights Movement. Accompanied by proud parents, wife and close friends, he travelled to the award ceremony in Oslo, Norway. During his second official address, he linked the non-violent movement in the United States to the need for the entire planet to surrender its dependence on weapons and warfare. Martin refused to keep any of the $50,000 that accompanied the prize, choosing to donate it to the SCLC and the other organizations that made up the Council for United Civil Rights Leadership (CUCRL).

During the 1957 Prayer Pilgrimage to Washington, D.C., Martin Luther King had made a plea that the federal government support black people's right to unfettered access to the ballot. The new Civil Rights Bill did not secure equal access to the ballot. So King and the SCLC

ABOVE RIGHT: **Martin King** with President John F. Kennedy in 1962. Ralph Bunche is seen here to King's left, and A. Philip Randolph stands next to Kennedy.

RIGHT: **This car was outside** the Sixteenth Street Baptist Church when a bomb tore through the wall. Four girls – Carole Robertson, Cynthia Wesley, Addie Mae Collins, and Denise McNair – were killed.

began searching for a way to get the question of voting rights before the national eye.

Some southern states had "understanding" clauses. These required registrants to interpret a section of the state constitution after it was read to them. Other states required payment of a fee to vote, called a poll tax. That kept sharecroppers and other poor people from voting. Whites were often exempt because the laws allowed those to vote whose ancestors had voted before 1867.

While King and the SCLC looked for a target, in Selma, Alabama, the Dallas County Voting Rights League (DCVRL) held regular meetings about how to get voting rights for black people. The DCVRL was headed by Amelia Platts Boynton and her husband Bill, who had been working for years to help black people vote. In Selma, blacks had to fill out a long two-page form that was hard for a literate person to read and understand, and impossible for someone who could not read and write. Selma law also required that someone vouch for the black prospective voter. The voucher was usually a white person who said that this was a "good Negro" who could be considered for voting. Amelia and her husband helped people learn how to fill out the forms. But when her husband, a registered voter, started taking three and four black people at a time to the courthouse to vote, the registrar declared that he was "doing the wrong thing by bringing these large numbers of black people to register and vote."

In 1963, the Student Non-violent Coordinating Committee entered Selma, and began working with the League to assist them in furthering their plans. Their task was made all the harder when Judge James A. Hare, a state judge, issued an injunction that outlawed public meetings to discuss voting rights for blacks. Together with local activists, the SNCC made progress in increasing the courage and willingness of people to take a stand.

One of their exciting moments was on October 8, 1963, "Freedom Day." Over 300 of Selma's black people went to the courthouse to register to vote. Not even ten people were allowed into the courthouse to take the literacy test. They stood firm despite police harassing them, threatening to report to their employers that they were troublemakers. Led by Sheriff Jim Clark, police even went so far as to use cattleprods on people to scare them.

Those who dared to attend the mass meetings contended with police gathering around the meeting places, circling the cars and writing down license plate numbers to pass on to the White Citizens Council. People knew that the racist White Citizens Council could make life quite uncomfortable for them, causing them to lose their jobs, or worse. Amelia Boynton often received anonymous phone calls telling her to stop agitating or face being driven out of town.

Despite such threats and intimidation, the voting rights movement grew. Finally, in 1964, soon after King

LEFT: These people are lined up for voter registration in Fayette County, Tennessee. Protesters organized such "marches" to county courthouses because blacks were often not permitted to register.

RIGHT: King holds the Nobel Peace Prize, awarded to him in 1964. At 35 years old, he was the youngest person ever to receive the prestigious award. He saw the prize as a call to speak out on issues of world peace.

won the Nobel Prize, Amelia Boynton met with the SCLC to ask them to come to Selma.

On Monday, January 18, 1965, the SNCC and SCLC launched a combined campaign to bring voting rights to Selma. On that day, Martin Luther King and John Lewis of the SNCC led 400 marchers to the courthouse to register people to vote. Following Judge Hare's orders, Sheriff Jim Clark blocked the entrance to the courthouse, ordering the protesters to line up in an alleyway and wait. After several hours, not one person was registered to vote.

That first day, organizers were surprised at Clark's restraint. He didn't arrest a single protester. Known for his brutality, Clark embodied the violence that the SCLC knew revealed racism and hatred most effectively on the television screen for the nation to see. Although it may seem callous and calculating, the SCLC had learned that for protests to draw national attention, there had to be displays of extreme white violence. Recalling how Albany, Georgia's, Police chief Laurie Pritchett's show of moderation and restraint had obscured the racism in Albany, they realized Selma sheriff Jim Clark's shows of blatant brutality assisted their cause.

The next day, Clark performed. King and Lewis led another column of protesters to the courthouse, but this time they refused to stand in the alley. Clark ordered them to leave the sidewalk in front of the courthouse. When they didn't move as quickly as he thought they should, he started pushing and shoving them. Amelia Boynton stood glaring at him, her anger and disdain clear in her face. Clark grabbed her by the collar, and shoved her half a block to the police car. The sight of Clark shaking her limp body down the street received national attention.

A few days later, on January 22, 1965, over 100 black teachers carried out a silent vigil to the courthouse. Sheriff Clark and his force cruelly jabbed people with cattleprods and clubs. His attack against the teachers fed the black community's anger, leading to more and more people joining the protests.

J.L. Chestnut, a black lawyer trained at Howard University in Washington, D.C., who worked for the NAACP Legal Defense Fund, helped get people out of jail in Selma when they were arrested en masse during the marches to the courthouse. At first, Chestnut disagreed with King's strategy of trying the case in the "courts of public opinion"

LEFT: Invited by the Dallas County (Alabama) Voters Rights League, King arrived in Selma in January 1965 to join efforts with the SNCC and the DCVRL. Here he offers inspiring words in an evening rally to urge people to continue protesting. The next day they marched on the Dallas County Courthouse.

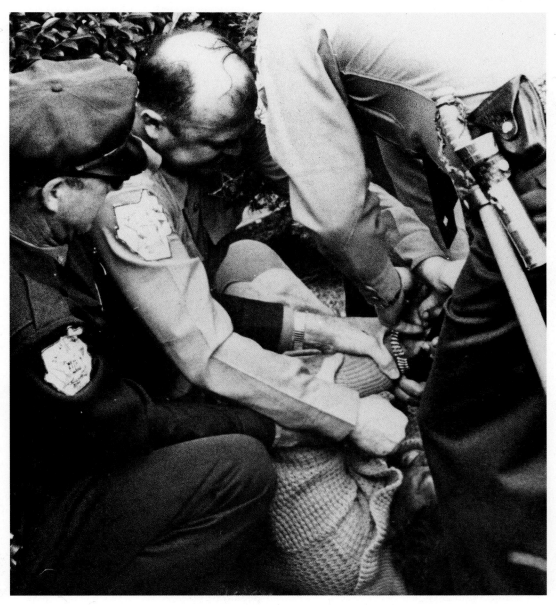

RIGHT: Sheriff Jim Clark wrestles a black woman to the ground outside the Dallas County Courthouse. Clark had pushed her, and she responded by punching him in the head.

LEFT: King leads a crowd in prayer after their arrest in Selma on February 1, 1965. After the prayer, they stood and marched off to jail.

RIGHT: King speaks at the funeral of Jimmie Lee Jackson, 26, who was killed during a demonstration for voting rights in Marion, Alabama.

instead of the legal courts. Yet he, like many other people at that time, soon realized that legal strategies worked best in tandem with the massive public pressure created by the direct action.

Chestnut recalled King's behavior during weekly meetings to discuss strategies. A supreme mediator, Martin always spoke last. Listening attentively to everyone's arguments, he observed their emotions. His own face remained expressionless. Finally, he'd stand, summarizing all the points made, acknowledging pros and cons. After measuring the proposals against the campaign's goals, he would say what proposal he preferred, and start planning next steps. According to Chestnut, King brought together "ministers, gangsters, self-seekers, students, prima donnas, and devoted high-minded people."

The SCLC decided that it was time to raise the stakes in Selma. On Monday, February 1, they marched in such large numbers that they purposely violated the city's parade ordinance. King led the march and was arrested along with more than 200 others.

While in jail, King wrote a letter that appeared in the *New York Times* explaining why he was in jail. He asked readers if, in order to vote, they had been forced to answer 100 questions on government issues so obscure that even political scientists would have trouble interpreting them. The letter stated that in Selma, Alabama, more blacks were in jail fighting for the right to vote than were on the voting rolls.

Protests continued while King was in jail. And Sheriff Clark continued to make arrests. King was released on February 5th.

On February 18, 1965, a march evolved in nearby Marion, Alabama, to go to the jail to protest the arrest of James Orange, one of the SCLC organizers. State troopers were sent in to stop the protesters, frightening them with abuse. Albert Turner, one of the rally's planners, recalled that police abuse was used because city officials believed that if "they would beat us up, . . . we were supposed to stop after the good whipping." During the clash, Jimmie Lee Jackson, a young man newly involved in the protests, threw himself over his mother to protect her from the blows raining down on her. State troopers shot him dead. Outraged, people began rumbling about taking Jimmie Lee's body to Montgomery and dumping it on Governor George Wallace's desk.

King and the SCLC incorporated that anger and energy into a plan to march from Selma to Montgomery to demand voting rights and an end to the brutality.

On Sunday, March 7, 1965, hundreds gathered at Brown Chapel to begin the march. Many of the marchers came from Marion, Alabama, the site of the murder of Jimmie Lee Jackson. Organizers were sure that Governor Wallace would not allow the march to take place. King had flown back to Atlanta to deliver service at his church, so Hosea Williams of the SCLC and John Lewis of the SNCC together led the march. When the front line crossed the Edmund Pettus Bridge, the marchers were stopped by helmet-clad state troopers who were armed with rifles and batons. Lewis recalled a "Major Cloud" saying that the march was unlawful. The crowd was given three minutes to disperse. Instead everyone kneeled down to pray. Three minutes had not passed before the Major called for the troopers to advance.

The troopers mowed the protesters down. Tear gas

ABOVE: On March 7, 1965, demonstrators set out to march from Montgomery to Selma. State troopers would not allow them to march over the Edmund Pettus Bridge. Here SNCC leader John Lewis wards off blows on "Bloody Sunday."

LEFT: Two days later, another column of marchers set out from Brown Chapel to cross the Edmund Pettus Bridge. Marchers came from around the country, black and white, in answer to the call for justice.

RIGHT: King leads marchers on the second day of the Selma-to-Montgomery march, March 22, 1965. Ralph Abernathy is at right.

poisoned the air, and in a panic, people ran, coughing and vomiting as mounted police beat them from above. The terror continued all the way to the Chapel. Surrounded by a black community not pledged to non-violence, the troopers fled the scene. The Chapel was turned into a hospital to take care of people's injuries. Nationally televised, "Bloody Sunday" sent shock waves across the continent.

Profoundly upset, King issued a call to people of good will to join the marchers in Selma. Among those who answered the call were 450 clergy from around the country. This time, the state had been able to get a federal injunction that said that people could not march. On March 9th, King led the demonstrators to the bridge. Once again, police ordered them to turn around. Ralph Aber-

nathy led the group in prayer. King led the people in retreat. Many expressed shock that he would do that, because they were prepared to stay and face the police violence again. But King felt that he could not disobey a federal injunction, even though lawyer William Kunstler said that it was an illegal injunction that could not stand up to a challenge.

That night, three of the out-of-state ministers that had joined the march lost their way returning to their hotel. Attacked by six whites, one of the men was so badly injured that he never regained consciousness. Episcopal minister and AFSC worker James Reeb's death intensified the outrage over the situation in Selma.

On March 13, 1965, Governor Wallace met with Presi-

LEFT: On March 25, 1965, a crowd of at least 30,000 congregated at the Alabama state capitol calling for equal access to the ballot. Governor George Wallace refused to see the demonstrators.

BELOW: After the passage of the 1965 Voting Rights Act propelled by massive demonstrations and civil disobedience, rural Alabama saw black people voting by the thousands. Here prospective voters stand in line to vote.

dent Lyndon B. Johnson. Wallace refused to protect marchers, saying that he was unable to do so. Proclaiming that the marchers had a constitutional right to proceed, Johnson federalized Alabama state troops in order to protect them. Two days later, Johnson addressed the U.S. Congress in a televised meeting, with 70 million Americans watching. He declared that all Americans had a right to vote. Calling on Congress to delay no longer, he announced the Voting Rights Bill that would eliminate obstacles to blacks voting. He amazed the nation by ending his speech with the words, "We shall overcome."

On the 21st of March, 1965, King led the victorious marchers on the five-day, 54-mile trek from Selma to Montgomery, Alabama. The crowd of 8000 that started out became more than 25,000 strong by the time it reached the state capital. Outside the state capital, a massive rally was held, with entertainers and speakers. When King spoke, he reached out his arms, looking at the great body of people that surrounded him, and congratulated the people for their steadfastness. He reminded them that there were those who said that they would never carry out that march to Montgomery, yet here they were. He said that the people were on the move, and that nothing would turn them back. In a mighty call that invoked the four-fold refrain of Psalm 13, King answered the question, "How long will it take?" Four times he asked the question, and each time, he shouted an answer that lifted the soul and assured the heart that no matter what, the march of justice could not be halted. Indeed, he said, the universe itself backed their fight, and the Lord himself would never abandon them.

It was the largest civil rights demonstration ever held in the South. By the end of that summer, 9000 black people of Selma had registered to vote.

CHAPTER 5

TAKING THE MOVEMENT NORTH

Just two weeks after President Johnson signed the 1965 Voting Rights Act into law, Watts erupted in a fiery outbreak of anger. For five days, this suburb outside of Los Angeles burned. Tanks patrolled the streets as 14,000 National Guardsmen swarmed the streets, demanding identification, setting up checkpoints, and enforcing martial law. Thirty-four people died and 4000 people were arrested.

Watts was not the first race riot in the 1960s. In 1963, after the Birmingham agreement between city officials, merchants and the black community, fighting broke out instigated by whites who started bombing and terrifying black people. In 1964 riots broke out in Harlem and Rochester, New York, triggered by killings of black individuals. The Watts riot was triggered by the arrest of a black man, Marquette Frye.

These scattered fires of anger and disillusionment had come to Martin Luther King's attention, and he looked to the March on Washington as a way to rechannel that energy, and to give people hope. But the Watts riot rocked the nation because it lasted so long, and the damage to life and property was so extensive.

Deeply disturbed by the riots, King decided to tour Watts, talking to black leaders, city officials and residents to see if he could understand the cause of the riots. He was shocked to find out that many of the young people saw him and his theories of non-violence as irrelevant. In fact, many of the people that had participated in the riots were proud – proud because they had forced the government to pay attention.

In a conversation with Bayard Rustin after that trip, the heartbroken King offered a metaphor: after working so hard to get the people the right to eat hamburgers, now he'd have to get them the money to eat those hamburgers!

In his article that appeared in the *Saturday Review*, "Next Stop: The North," Martin apologized for his lack of awareness regarding the conditions brewing in the northern ghettoes. Saying that unemployment and pitiful wages are at the root of ghetto misery, he vowed to search for a program founded on non-violence to address these pressing problems.

Accusing the California state government of contributing to conditions that led to the Watts crisis, he reminded readers that in 1964, California was the first state to repeal a law that forbade housing discrimination. The Watts riots fired King's resolve to find a northern city in which to demonstrate the feasibility of non-violent campaigns to resolve the problems faced by blacks in the North. After considering Philadelphia, New York, Cleveland, Washington, and Chicago, King and the SCLC decided on Chicago.

Chicago was the second largest city in the United

ABOVE RIGHT: President Lyndon B. Johnson and Martin Luther King, Jr. shake hands after Johnson signs the 1965 Voting Rights Act.

RIGHT: Watts burns for five days during rioting sparked by a confrontation between a black person and the police.

States and was one-quarter black. Many of the black people in Chicago had migrated there from Mississippi in search of jobs.

Al Raby and the Coordinating Council of Community Organizations (CCCO) in Chicago paved the way for King to enter the city. Created in 1962 to combat school segregation policies in Chicago, the CCCO joined the West Side Federation, the Woodlawn Organization, and local chapters of the Urban League, the NAACP, CORE, and SNCC. In 1963 they joined cities around the country in launching a series of student boycotts. Two hundred thousand students stayed out of Chicago schools in protest.

The campaign launched by the CCCO and SCLC focused on discrimination in housing. Chicago's segregated housing system was maintained by real estate agents capitalizing on and amplifying prejudices that already existed. They carefully monitored who they sold houses to, making sure that neighborhoods remained all-black or all-white. Real estate agents ushered black people into housing that was poorly maintained, overcrowded, and more expensive than housing for whites.

In January 1966, Martin moved into one of these tenements. He and Coretta discovered personally the truth of the poor housing conditions. Coretta recalled her alarm when she saw that apartment. The landlord had hurriedly cleaned and painted the apartment when he learned that Martin Luther King was moving in, but it still did not measure up to housing codes. The hallway floors were unfinished, with only one dingy light in the hallway, shabby stairs, and a dangerously rickety fire escape. The refrigerator did not work once it was filled with food. For this Martin paid $90/month unfurnished. Nicer larger apartments in white sections of Chicago were $80/month.

In the summer of 1966, Coretta and Martin brought their four children to their dreary two-bedroom apartment. The children had nowhere to play but the street; not even the park had a trace of greenery. With alarm, they saw their normally well-balanced, mannerly children become sullen and disobedient as the oppressive atmosphere of the ghetto seeped into their spirits.

On July 10, 1966, King led a high-spirited rally at Soldier Field attended by 50,000 people. After reading the demands which included a call for open housing, the people marched to City Hall where Martin tacked the demands to the entrance.

The Chicago campaign started off with an effort to clean up and renovate the black neighborhoods in order to boost morale and encourage the people that change could come to Chicago. The organizers also wanted to publicize Mayor Richard Daley's neglect of the poorer

ABOVE LEFT: King talks to people in the Watts area of Los Angeles. He was disappointed to learn that they found his non-violent approach to change ineffective.

LEFT: These people are demonstrating for an end to segregated housing in Chicago. This was hard to attack because the segregated system was maintained by a system of real estate practices.

RIGHT: The Kings speak with reporters about their reasons for moving into a slum flat in Chicago. They wanted to expose how the poor living conditions in black apartment buildings were maintained by neglectful landlords.

neighborhoods. Time after time, their plan backfired, for when Daley discovered their plans to clean up a particular site, he deployed one of his own crews there first.

Daley was not about to fall into the trap that the southern officials had fallen into – allowing the Civil Rights Movement to make an example out of their brutality. In 1963, Daley had held a huge fundraiser for the 1963 Birmingham campaign. He knew the strategy of the Movement all too well. Therefore, whenever the organizers made demands, he offered suave and well thought out answers.

King, however, did not understand Daley's strategy. He did not realize that many of his allies for the campaigns in the South were no longer allies when he moved north. Jesse Jackson, then on the staff of the SCLC, described that there were ministers and classmates of King's on Daley's payroll. This payroll was the corrupt Daley machinery, a system of passing out favors in exchange for votes and support.

A couple of days after the march to Soldier Field, a riot broke out in Chicago. As usual on a very hot day in the city, young people were playing in water they sent spraying from the fire hydrants. When police demanded that they turn off the hydrants, a melee ensued. Daley blamed the

ABOVE: These whites gather to jeer and intimidate black demonstrators who are demanding open housing in Chicago and surrounding neighborhoods.

RIGHT: On August 7, 1966, King and Chicago Campaign organizers leave a meeting with city officials who are trying to persuade them to stop the housing protests. The organizers refused.

riots on King and the SCLC, calling them outsiders who came in and incited people, then weren't able to control them after they became incensed.

Martin and the CCCO shifted the focus of their Chicago campaign from renovating the black neighborhoods to challenging the closed housing system. They marched on Gage Park, a segregated white neighborhood. The whites screamed and shouted at them, throwing stones and bricks, burning and overturning cars. Andrew Young remembers being more frightened of the raging white people in Chicago than he had been of the whites screaming at them in the South.

On August 25, 1966, Mayor Daley and Martin King signed a ten-point agreement. In that agreement, King

agreed to call off the marches and demonstrations in exchange for negotiations regarding fair housing and changes in the Chicago policies. Within the CCCO alliance, many of the grassroots organizers were sorely disappointed. They were angry that they had been excluded from discussions, and that the agreement had not yet yielded a fair housing bill.

Because King had not succeeded in representing the desires of many of the organizers, the marches through white neighborhoods continued. On September 4th, black people marched through Cicero, a staunchly white neighborhood that black people avoided after dark to protect their lives. Even though 15,000 blacks worked in Cicero, none lived there.

After the daunting Chicago campaign, King found himself at a critical juncture. During the campaign, he had joined the Memphis-to-Jackson freedom march. Organized by the SNCC, CORE and SCLC to resume the march halted by James Meredith when he was shot, King found himself facing growing differences within the Civil Rights Movement. Long-time allies, the SNCC and CORE now consisted of young people who rejected King's vision of non-violence as the only tactic to achieve liberation.

One of the strategies of the Movement, the calling in of whites as allies to put their bodies on the line together with black people, had become a source of deep pain. The murders of white people drew the outrage of whites in America in a way that the murders of black people never did. Resentment grew as young black activists saw white people taking control in black organizations, and yet the white community as a whole still refused to accept blacks as equals.

During this march, King faced the call to "Black Power." The call reflected black people's desire to take control of their own social, political and economic institutions. And sometimes it meant a call for justice no matter what the cost. Integration no longer seemed viable, and black people wanted just to have control of their own.

Martin suffered deeply over the divisions, and the refutation of non-violence. Like a father who feels wounded when his children reject his sacrifices as inadequate, he pitied himself. Yet he emerged out of this selfish thinking

ABOVE: Marchers near the end of the 220-mile "March Against Fear" from Memphis, Tennessee, to Jackson, Mississippi, in June 1966. The black panther was chosen as a symbol because it fights back if attacked.

ABOVE RIGHT: King and Malcolm X met only once, in 1964. By 1966, Martin heard echoes of Malcolm's black nationalist call for justice "by any means necessary" all around him.

RIGHT: A black soldier in Vietnam waits for the rest of his squad. King spoke out firmly against the Vietnam War.

ABOVE: This picture of King at Highlander Center was used as propaganda that King was a Communist, in an attempt to discredit both Highlander and King.

LEFT: King realized that desegregation and voting rights were not enough to redress past injustices. He began to focus on economic inequities such as inadequate resources for black children.

RIGHT: Garbage workers on strike wear signs pointing out that they are demanding more than increased wages and union recognition — they want to be treated with respect. King supported their fight because he saw economic reform as the key to equality in the United States.

place. Instead of responding to the allegation on a professional level, Hoover ordered surveillance of King's hotel rooms and his home to find out if he had any Communist links. While the FBI was unable to uncover any evidence that King's closest companions were Communist, they did discover that King had extra-marital relationships. They tried to use this information to injure Martin and his family as well as to discredit him internationally.

Bernard Lee, one of the SCLC staff, described an incident that stung King into condemning the Vietnam War. Returning from Jamaica, King was flipping through *Ramparts* magazine when a picture illustrating an article on Vietnam struck him still. The picture depicted a Vietnamese woman holding her dead baby, a victim of napalming by U.S. soldiers. From then until he died, 16 months later, King was one of the most prominent opponents of the war in Vietnam.

He denounced the war in Vietnam nationally at Riverside Church in New York City on April 4, 1967, exactly one year before his death. The NAACP, as well as other black leaders, were infuriated by his stance against the war. They believed that it threatened the Civil Rights Movement and the possibility of more gains for black people.

The *New York Times* and *Washington Post* editorials criticized his stance. *Life* magazine called the speech "an advertisement for Radio Hanoi." Carl Rowan (black columnist and former director of the United States Information Agency) called King "utterly irresponsible." Andrew Young, one of King's closest aides, saw the response as a thinly veiled way of saying "nigger, stay in your place."

As a Nobel Peace Prize winner, King felt justified in speaking out on issues of international peace. He answered the criticisms against him by reminding people that he was a minister before he was a civil rights leader. And answering the call of God meant being willing to stand alone, and doing that which was right.

In the winter of 1967, King's soul was battle-weary. Coping with criticism from all sides because of the incomplete victory against discriminatory housing in Chicago and his denouncement of the war in Vietnam, he did his best to stay focused on next steps.

In his memoirs, Ralph Abernathy described an event that deeply shook the two of them, and fuelled King's vision for next steps. In 1968, they visited a small schoolhouse in Marks, Mississippi. They chatted with the schoolteacher, asking her how she was able to help the children to succeed when they had so many obstacles to hurdle. During the conversation, the teacher excused herself to feed the children lunch. Abernathy and King watched, their eyes growing larger, as she gave each child an apple quarter and a few crackers. Slowly it dawned on them that the children were underweight, and that was all the food that they would have for lunch. When the two men left, Martin was crying. He told Ralph that he hadn't really understood that many schoolchildren were slowly starving in the United States.

Refusing to fall victim to the "politics of despair," he issued a call for the Poor People's Campaign in December 1967. He envisioned thousands of poor people from all over the country – black, white, Puerto Rican, Mexican American, Latino, and Native American – travelling to the

nation's capital, demanding decent jobs and respect. He wanted all of America to see and hear about what people really experienced.

While organizing for the Poor People's Campaign, King reminded people of the findings of the President's Commission on Civil Disorders. So alarmed by the many outbreaks of unrest in the nation's cities, Johnson charged the Commission with finding out the cause of the riots, and how to stop them. The March 1968 report said that, "Our nation is splitting into two hostile societies and the chief destructive cutting force is white racism."

The findings, arrived at by a very conservative committee, confirmed what King had been saying all along. He warned listeners that racism was a crippling force that hobbled America's desires to be fully democratic and true to its finest ideals.

Meanwhile, King received another call. Black garbage workers in Memphis, Tennessee, were on strike, and his colleague the Reverend James Lawson wanted him to come to support them.

The black workers had made constant unanswered pleas to the city for worker's compensation, higher wages, and sound equipment. When two men died, crushed by a malfunctioning trash compactor, 1300 men said "no more."

Memphis's black community staunchly supported the garbage workers. They saw the poor treatment the workers received as symptomatic of the lack of respect given to black people as a whole in Memphis. Mayor Henry Loeb refused to negotiate with the workers, and everywhere he went the white community praised him for his firm rejection of the unionization of black workers.

On March 18, 1968, King went to Memphis to speak. Affirming the rightness of the fight, he said that it was a crime to live in a wealthy nation and receive starvation wages. Looking around him at the hundreds that packed the auditorium, he advised them to call for a general work stoppage. He promised to return to Memphis in ten days and lead a mass demonstration.

King returned to Memphis just in time to lead the demonstration. Just a mile away, a fight had broken out between some black people and the police. When a young girl was injured, people started passing the word that she had been killed.

King led the march, the mood turning sour as people learned the rumor. Behind him, he heard windows crashing, and screams. The march had become a riot.

Deeply saddened, Martin feared that the media would say that he was no longer able to lead a non-violent demonstration. He worried that the upcoming Poor People's Campaign would be challenged on the basis of fears that violence would occur.

Determined to lead a non-violent march in Memphis, he returned on April 3rd. In a nearly prophetic speech, he called on America to be true to what was written on paper, and to live out the meaning of democracy. Recalling the changes he had seen since the onset of the Montgomery Bus Boycott, he sang out that he no longer feared for his life, because he had been to the mountaintop, and had seen the Promised Land. Martin King had faith that with or without him, the movement would continue.

He was shot and killed the next day, April 4th, while standing on the balcony of the Lorraine Hotel in Memphis. The Poor People's Campaign was set to begin on April 22, 1968.

LEFT: On April 3, 1968, King stands on the balcony of the Lorraine Hotel with Jesse Jackson and Ralph Abernathy. The next day he was shot and killed as he stood in the same place.

BELOW: Thousands mourn King's death at Ebenezer Baptist Church. Although James Earl Ray was convicted of the killing, further evidence suggests FBI involvement.

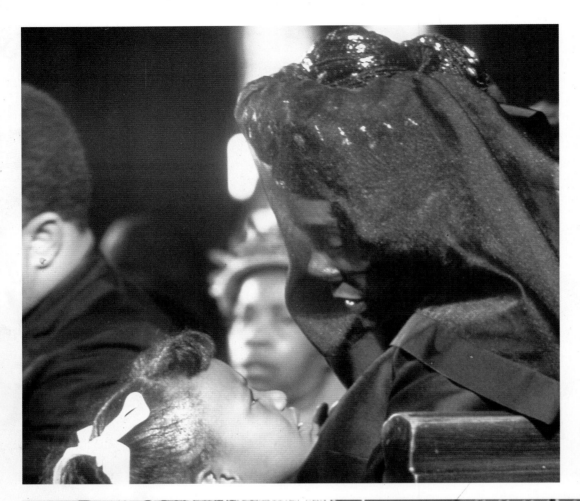

LEFT: Coretta Scott King and daughter Yolanda at King's funeral.

BELOW: A mule-drawn wagon pulls King's coffin through the streets of Atlanta on April 8, 1968, as thousands march in sorrow.

RIGHT: At the Southview Cemetery, members of the King family mourn. Shown are Yolanda King, who holds her little sister Bernice on her lap; Martin III; Coretta; and singer Harry Belafonte (right), family friend and SCLC supporter.

BELOW: Mourners walk the five miles from Ebenezer Baptist Church to Morehouse College, where another service is held.

CHAPTER 6

THE NEVER-ENDING CALL

Although King died, the struggle continued. Within Memphis, white clergy joined with black people to support the rights of the garbage workers to negotiate for fair wages. Thousands of people from around the nation joined Coretta Scott King and the SCLC as they kept Martin's pledge to hold a non-violent march in support of the workers. In a silent vigil – the only sound shoe leather against the pavement – they marched to Memphis's City Hall. Mayor Loeb agreed to negotiate, and on April 14th, the garbage workers won their right to have a union, resulting in higher wages, workman's compensation, a grievance procedure, and respect.

The Poor People's Campaign continued. Starting on May 11, 1968, black, white, Native-American, Mexican-American, and Puerto Rican poor streamed into Washington, D.C. Thousands came by foot, by bus, by car and by mule. Setting up tents outside, they created Resurrection City, complete with a day care center, newspaper, and running water. The SCLC, led by Ralph Abernathy, worked together with countless organizations to coordinate this unprecedented gathering of the nation's poor.

On the marches, Mexican-Americans, Native Americans and African-Americans shared and compared their particular struggles and needs, realizing that while they had much in common, their needs and histories differed greatly. In Washington, poor people packed the government chambers as they met with representatives of the government departments to voice their demands and describe the realities of their lives.

The demands made through the Campaign were partially answered. Federal agencies such as the departments of Agriculture, Housing and Urban Development, and Labor agreed to change discriminatory practices, and to increase programs that alleviated poverty.

Yet the Poor People's Campaign died in clouds as U.S. Park Service police tear-gassed the men, women and children of Resurrection City on June 23rd, and heavily armed Washington police drove out residents the next day, just six weeks after it started.

King's death on April 4, 1968, was not the end of a movement, just as his life was not the beginning of a movement. However, the accumulated deaths of John F. Kennedy, Malcolm X, civil rights leader Medgar Evers, and Martin Luther King, closely followed by the death of Robert Kennedy, was steadily corroding the hearts of many of the people taking a stand for themselves. As the U.S. government responded to internal dissension with martial law and surveillance, dreams shrivelled.

The Civil Rights Movement radically altered the structure of American society. It forced states to strike down legal barriers that prevented black people access to schools and public facilities. It revolutionized voting rights. Many black people no longer faced the same bold-faced terror that they did before the movement's apex.

Martin's legacy is the method by which he brought about change, and his unwillingness to ever give up non-violence as the way to make sure that the means was in concert with the ends desired.

ABOVE: Resurrection City was created by thousands of poor people who marched, drove, and rode mules to the nation's capital to let the voices of the poor be heard. The Poor People's Campaign began on May 11, 1968.

RIGHT: Ralph Abernathy, the head of SCLC after King's death, addresses the people of Resurrection City.

Yet Martin Luther King's larger dream, evolving in the later years of his life, was a dream that poverty be abolished. In his last book, *Where Do We Go From Here* (1967), he outlines a program that includes a guaranteed income for all. He showed that this program for life would be less costly than the program for war and death. He stressed that true democracy could not be achieved until there were no longer haves and have nots. That dream has not yet been realized.

Memorials for King are numerous. Monuments, commemorative stamps, buildings and streets bearing his name and museums honor his memory. Yet perhaps the memorials that are most fitting are the living memorials – the people who continue to walk and make waves in the spirit of his vision for a peace that is justice.

Bernice Johnson Reagon, former activist of the Albany, Georgia, movement and now curator of he Museum of American History at the Smithsonian Institution, speaks of the power awakened in so many people as they participated in the Civil Rights Movement.

ABOVE: **1986** marked the first national observance of Martin Luther King, Jr.'s memory. Vice President George Bush and South African bishop Desmond Tutu join Coretta Scott King at a wreath-laying ceremony at King's crypt.

RIGHT: The Civil Rights Memorial at Southern Poverty Law Center in Montgomery, Alabama.

You can see how that power fueled Jesse Jackson and the Rainbow Coalition. You can see how that power fueled John Lewis, now a Congressional representative. You can see how that power fueled Marion Wright Edelman who is now director of the Children's Defense Fund. But there are millions who that power fueled, and you cannot see it so clearly. But it is there.

That movement fueled the social, cultural and political understandings of millions of people, both within the United States and internationally. It fueled those whose

DR. MARTIN LUTHER KING JR.
ASSASINATED. MEMPHIS, TN

3 OCT. 1967

SAMUEL HAMMOND JR. DELANO
MIDDLETON HENRY SMITH. STUDENTS
KILLED WHEN HIGHWAY PATROLMEN
FIRED ON PROTESTERS. ORANGEBURG, SC

THURGOOD MARSHALL SWORN IN AS FIRST
BLACK SUPREME COURT JUSTICE

12 MAY. 1967
BENJAMIN BROWN. CIVIL RIGHTS WORKER
KILLED WHEN POLICE FIRED ON PROTESTERS
JACKSON, MS

1967
WHARLEST JACKSON. CIVIL RIGHTS LEADER
KILLED AFTER PROMOTION TO 'WHITE' JOB
NATCHEZ, MS

CLARENCE TRIGGS. SLAIN BY NIGHTRIDERS
BOGALUSA, LA

BEN CHESTER WHITE. KILLED BY KLAN
NATCHEZ, MS

VERNON DAHMER BLACK COMMUNITY
LEADER KILLED IN KLAN BOMBING
HATTIESBURG, MS

SAMUEL YOUNGE JR. STUDENT CIVIL RIGHTS
ACTIVIST KILLED IN DISPUTE OVER 'WHITES
ONLY' RESTROOM. TUSKEGEE, AL

JONATHAN DANIELS. SEMINARY STUDE
KILLED BY DEPUTY. HAYNEVILLE, AL

WILLIE WALLACE BREWSTER. K
NIGHTRIDERS. ANNISTON, AL

SES VO

LEFT: A crowd of 55,000 attended the 25th Anniversary of the March on Washington in August of 1988. The march focused on eliminating poverty and joblessness, creating world peace and eradicating apartheid in South Africa.

RIGHT: Jesse Jackson addresses the 1988 March on Washington. In 1988, Jackson ran as a presidential candidate in the Democratic primaries.

RIGHT: March 7, 1990: Coretta Scott King and Jesse Jackson are among those that march across the Edmund Pettus Bridge in Selma, Alabama, 25 years after Bloody Sunday.

names may never be known, who marched, sang, boycotted, sat-in, died-in and died, protesting for right.

Mahatma Gandhi said, "I believe that if one man gains spiritually, the whole world gains with him, and if one man falls, the whole world falls to that extent."

Perhaps King's greatest gift was his ability to sense the reservoir of potential in everyone, to tap into that reservoir, and thereby to encourage people to rise to their best. He was not flawless, as none of us are flawless. Yet he was a model of what striving for spiritual justice and the moral high ground can mean. He shows that it is possible to be transformed and redeemed by listening to that which is around us, and to remain open to hearing the cries of the suffering, acknowledging our unbreakable links with and responsibilities to one another.

He calls on all of us to equate peace with justice, to understand that the quality of life is what matters most. When we wonder if this is enough, we can recall his words, "Everybody can be great. Because everybody can serve. You don't have to have a college degree to serve. You don't have to make your subject and verb agree to serve. You don't have to know about Plato and Aristotle . . . [or] Einstein's theory of relativity . . . to serve. You only need a heart full of grace. A soul generated by love."

BELOW: These children attend a memorial honoring Dr. King's life and legacy on January 15, 1987, the 58th anniversary of his birth.

RIGHT: King speaks to 30,000 marchers in front of the Alabama State Capitol, March 25, 1965. Years after his death, King's message of the interrelatedness of all people's destinies still rings true.

INDEX

Page numbers in *italics* indicate illustrations

PICTURE CREDITS

All photographs courtesy of UPI/Bettmann Newsphotos, except the following:
Collection of Tina Bristol: 26(both), 27, 28, 29.
Brompton Photo Library: 3, 64(top).
Boston University, Special Collections, Mugar Memorial Library: 13(bottom).
Highlander Research and Education Center, New Market, TN: 31(bottom).
New England Stock: Jean Higgins: 7(bottom left), 10-11, 75; Jim Schwabel: 2, 14, 15.
United States Army Photograph: 63(bottom).
Wadsworth Atheneum, Amistad Foundation, Photography by David Stansbury: 10(top).
Wide World: 68.